MATCHING & NUMBERS

MELANIE RICE

ILLUSTRATED BY
CHRIS BARKER

ADVISER
BETTY ROOT

Kingfisher Books

Kingfisher Books, Grisewood & Dempsey Ltd,
Elsley House, 24–30 Great Titchfield Street, London W1P 7AD.

This edition published in 1990.
Originally published in hardcover in 1985 by Kingfisher Books as
part of a one-volume book entitled *Play Together Learn Together*.

BRITISH LIBRARY CATALOGUING IN PUBLICATION DATA
Rice, Melanie
Matching & numbers.
1. Activities for pre-school children — Manuals — For parents
1. Title II. Series
790.1'922

ISBN 0 86272 502 X

Printed in Spain.

Editor: Jacqui Bailey
Assistant Editor: Deri Robins
Design: The Pinpoint Design Company
Photography: Rex Caves
Cover Design: Nigel Osborne
Cover Photography: Mark French

Acknowledgements:
The author would like to thank her husband, Chris, for all his
invaluable advice and support during the preparation of this book.
The publishers would like to thank the staff and pupils of Hadrian
Lower School, Dunstable, for their help with some of the projects in
this book.

Contents

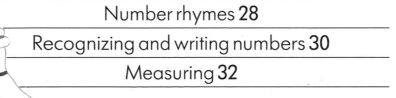

To parents

The 'Play Together, Learn Together' series is a compilation of ideas drawn from my experience of bringing up two young children. It was then that I discovered first hand just how long the hours can seem between breakfast and bedtime! With household chores and demanding minds competing for my attention all day, I usually found that despite good intentions, a backward glance showed how very little of my time was spent actually playing with the children. I hope that these books will provide parents who also have 'good intentions' with a source of reference; inspiring them to make the most of the rewarding hours spent in the company of their pre-school children.

Parent and Child Together

As the series title suggests, play should always be to the mutual benefit of child and parent. Parents learn a great deal about their children by observing them while they play and by listening to them recalling their experiences. Listening is particularly important; while it is easy to talk to children, listening requires more patience — it's all too tempting to interrupt or finish sentences which seem to falter or stray from the point.

Children learn from their parents through conversation as well as through other stimuli — poems, pictures, games and so on. And because of the special intimacy which exists between parent and child each activity can be directly related to the world they share.

But do remember that the emphasis in these books is on the word 'play'. Children learn much more quickly and easily when they are absorbed and interested in what they are doing. Never force your children into an activity; if they begin to get bored, do something else. Children are also quick to pick up on the moods of their parents, so if you are bored that is another good reason to do something else.

Using This Book

In making the selection of activities for this book I have tried to include only those which are readily accessible, which generally need little preparation and use materials close to hand, and which do not require special outings to provide stimulation.

The activities have not been arranged according to age; this type of categorization seemed irrelevant to me, as every child has a different rate of development. No doubt you too will have been irritated by being told that a 'three-year-old should be able to ...' when it's clear that, whatever the activity, children proceed at their own pace. While no amount of pushing can force them to begin learning before they're ready, once they've started it is impossible to stop them.

What Will They Learn?

The ideas in this book have been designed to help children acquire a wide variety of skills, enabling them to explore and interpret the world for themselves.

Sorting. Grouping objects according to shape and colour or arranging them in order of size are activities that can be done anywhere (sorting buttons in the living room, pasta shapes in the kitchen, leaves in the garden). First maths skills will be acquired along the way.

Counting. Children quickly learn to recite the numbers one to ten but understanding counting takes a little longer. They begin through learning one to one correspondence (through tea parties, for example: 'one cup for Mum, one for Big Ted' and so on), then they are ready to start counting. Always choose items they can touch as they count.

Observation. Matching and sorting games increase powers of observation. Encourage children to look for numbers on things around them (clothes labels, food packets, car registrations, for example).

Language. Talking about numbers, shapes, size etc. increases mathematical vocabulary.

Manual skills. Handling small objects, cutting out shapes and drawing activities help children develop the coordination needed for writing.

A Few Tips

Before starting a play session, bear the following in mind:

1. Atmosphere — a happy relaxed atmosphere is essential if a child is going to benefit from the session.

2. Timing — a tired or hungry child will be inattentive, while interruptions spoil concentration.

3. Location — some activities need plenty of room, others are messy and mopping up equipment needs to be on hand.

During a session:

1. Encouragement — constant praise, even for the smallest achievement will help develop a child's confidence and ability to learn new things.

2. Striking a balance — it's not easy to sit back and watch children explore and discover without succumbing to the temptation of imposing one's own ideas in order to speed up the process. Yet only by probing for themselves can children come to a real understanding of the world. Try to work alongside the child rather than lead.

3. Pace — introduce new ideas slowly and carefully and give plenty of practice with any new skills.

4. Success — don't dwell on things which seem difficult. Instead, find something your child is comfortable with and can be positive about.

And afterwards:

Sharing — display the best work for friends and other members of the family to see and admire.

Finally, remember that for both of you the main thing is that the whole exercise should be tremendous fun.

Colour

1 Sort any group of objects into piles according to colour. For example, divide up the washing into dark and light clothes.

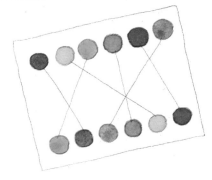

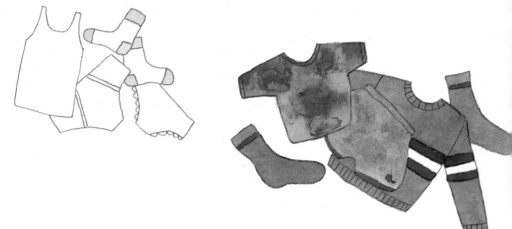

2 Paint six different colours on the left-hand side of a piece of paper and then put the same colours in a different order on the opposite side. Then match up the colours by joining them up with a pencil line. (Encourage you child to work from left to right as a preparation for reading.)

3 Draw two rows of six circles. Colour in the top six yourself but leave the others for your child to colour in matching shades.

4 Collect pictures from magazines. Cut a piece of colour from each picture. Mount the pictures onto card and match the coloured piece to the correct picture.

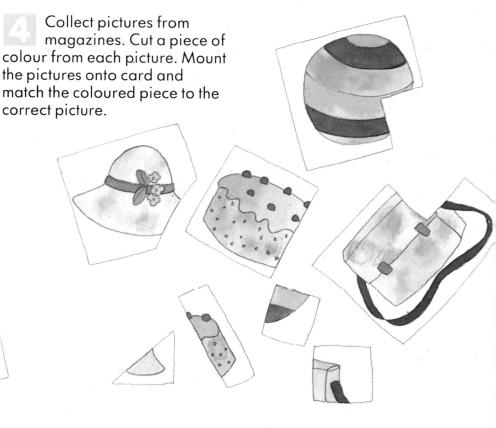

A colour game

Make a spinner out of a piece of card (see page 27) and divide it into six colours. Or, cover the six sides of a square wooden brick in a different colour for each side. Then divide a large sheet of stiff card into 20 squares. Colour in all the squares using the six colours on the spinner or brick. (Or, you can buy packets of gummed coloured squares and stick these onto the card instead.) Mark the 'Start' and 'Finish' boxes and stick or paint on a few arrows to show which direction the players move in. You will also need some counters.

To play—spin the spinner, or use the brick like a dice, and move your counter to the next square matching the colour the spinner has stopped on. Always move in the direction shown by the arrows. The winner is the first person to reach the 'Home' square by spinning the correct colour.

To make the game more fun, you could paste on some snakes and ladders as well

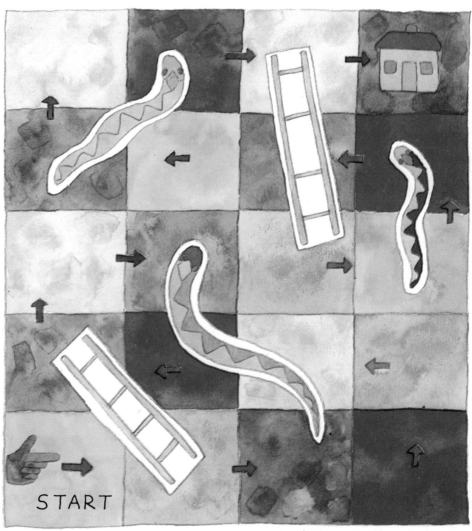

START

Shapes

1 Cut a piece of fruit in half and point out how each half matches in shape.

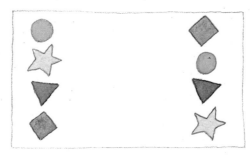

2 Fold a long piece of paper into pleats not less than 5 cm (2 ins) wide. Cut the pleated paper into any shape, but be careful to leave some of the edges on both sides uncut. Open out the paper and you should have a row of identical shapes.

3 Stick some simple shapes onto the left-hand side of a piece of paper (you can buy some boxes of gummed paper shapes, or see page 17 for some examples which you could trace). Stick the same shapes, but in a different order, onto the opposite side of the paper and join up the identical shapes with pencil lines.

4 Find an example of each of the solid shapes shown below and say what the names of the shapes are. Now look for other objects that have similar basic shapes.

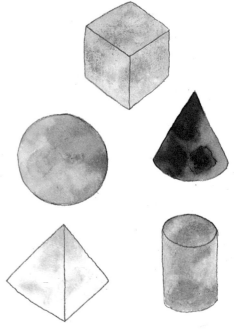

5 Draw four objects onto a piece of card. Make them very different in shape—for example, a pencil, a bottle, a cereal packet and a ball. Cut the pictures out. Now make four cards, each one showing a container that fits the shape of each of the objects. Make the shapes very simple, so that it will be easy for your child to match the bag to the object.

Two Little Dicky Birds
Two little dicky birds,
Sitting on the wall,
One named Peter,
The other named Paul.
Fly away Peter, fly away Paul.
Come back Peter, come back Paul.

(Traditional)

Sizes

Does your child understand words that indicate size, such as big, large, small, short, tall and long? Draw or glue pairs of pictures onto a large piece of paper to demonstrate the meaning of big and little, long and short, fat and thin. Talk about the pictures and put circles around the smallest, shortest and thinnest.

1 Make two cards—one bigger and one smaller. Write the words 'bigger' and 'smaller' on the cards—to help non-readers, make each word clearly match the size of the card.

Now take two objects that are the same shape but different sizes, such as a tablespoon and a teaspoon. Put the tablespoon on the 'bigger' card, and the teaspoon on the 'smaller' card. Use a variety of other objects as well, for example, a football and tennis ball; a 2p coin and a 1p coin; a big bowl and a small bowl. Sometimes put the smaller object down first, and sometimes the bigger, and put each pair down separately.

2 Collect several tins or pots of different sizes, each one with a lid. Take the lids off and mix them up. Put the right lid back on the right pot.

3 Collect a number of small objects and sort them into two piles—those that you think will fit into a matchbox and those that won't. Now find an empty matchbox and see if you are right.

4 Take a selection of toys and other objects and sort them into two piles—those that you think would fit through a letterbox and those that won't. Cut a hole the size of a letterbox into the side of a cardboard box. Now try 'posting' the things in your pile.

This game can also be played using holes of different shapes and sizes.

5 Line up a row of books of different heights on a flat piece of wood, or tabletop. Now arrange them in order of height.

Games to play

1 Draw three women, each one a different size and each on a separate sheet of paper. Arrange them in order of size.

2 Draw three potted plants, each one a different size, and arrange these in order.

Mix the two sets together, and then sort them so that the largest woman has the biggest plant, and so on.

3 Draw three vehicles, all with wheels of different sizes. Colour in the vehicles but not the wheels. Cut out some paper circles to match all the wheel sizes and colour them in to match the right vehicle. Stick the right wheels to the right vehicles.

Goldilocks and the three bears

Cut a sheet of card into 12 pieces. Draw each of the bears on three of the cards; their chairs on three others; their porridge bowls on three others and their beds on the last three. Each time, make one of the drawings large, one medium-sized and one small. Tell the story, holding up the cards as illustrations. Then play with the cards, sorting them by object and then by size.

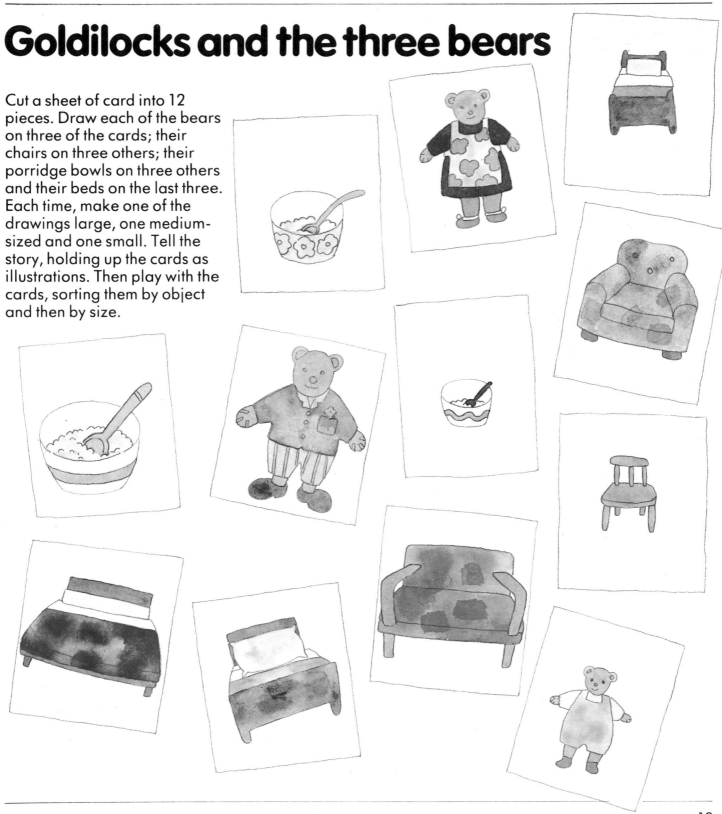

Things that go together

Shape Matching

Cut out some card templates of basic shapes (some examples are on page 17). Make up some pictures by drawing around the templates on a clean piece of paper. To complete the designs, give your child some ready-made shapes cut out from gummed coloured paper.

To make a game from this project, make up a few pictures on separate pieces of card using the outlines of only six different shapes. Then cut out a set of all the shapes needed to complete all the pictures and colour them in. Make a dice from a piece of firm card (see page 27) with each shape shown on one side of the dice.

Each player is given an outline picture.

The coloured shapes are spread out randomly over the table.

To play—the first player throws the dice. If the shape that falls uppermost on the dice matches one on his or her outline picture, the player picks up the matching piece from the coloured shapes and places it on their card. The winner is the first person to complete a picture.

14

Shadow Matching
Stick 12 clearly-outlined pictures onto thick card and cut them out. (Cheap colouring-in books are a good source for these kinds of pictures.) Take another piece of card and trace around each cut-out. Colour in the shapes with black. Now match the cut-out pictures to the shadow shapes.

Picture Pairs
Build up a collection of pictures of things that can be paired, such as a spider and its web, a telephone and its receiver, and so on. Muddle up all the pictures and then sort them into the correct pairs. You can also do this with real objects—like a knife and fork, cup and saucer, hairbrush and comb, etc.

Mix and muddle

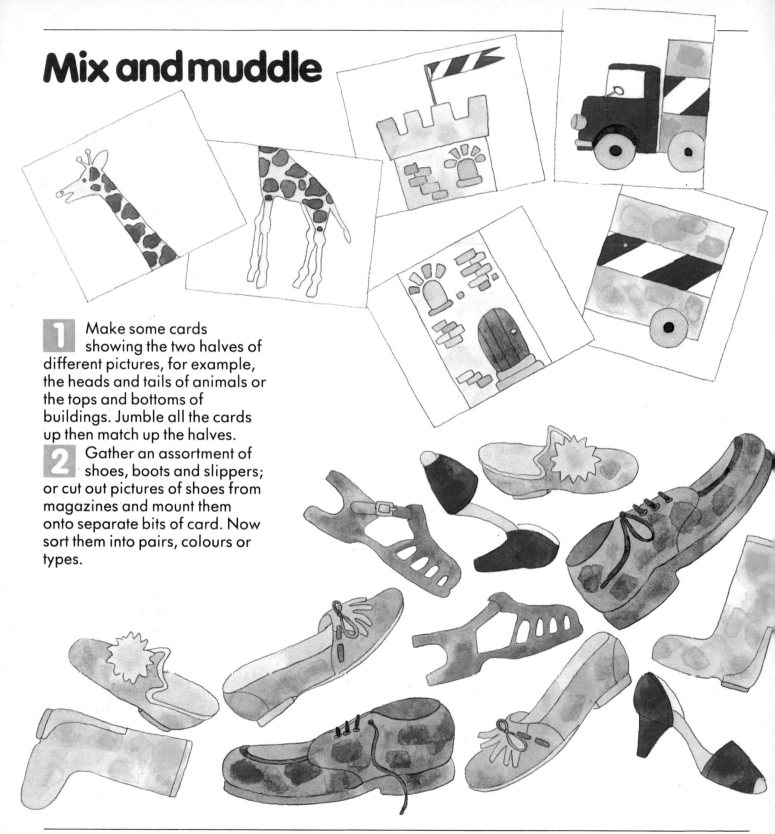

1 Make some cards showing the two halves of different pictures, for example, the heads and tails of animals or the tops and bottoms of buildings. Jumble all the cards up then match up the halves.

2 Gather an assortment of shoes, boots and slippers; or cut out pictures of shoes from magazines and mount them onto separate bits of card. Now sort them into pairs, colours or types.

Making your own cards

Cards can be used for all kinds of matching and pairing games. Whether you use letters, numbers or pictures on your cards depends on your child's knowledge and ability. Choose simple shapes and pictures for a young child, and clearly-written numbers, letters and simple words for a child learning to count and read.

There are some suggestions for games on the following pages, but first, here are a few general hints about making cards.

Recommended card size
Make your cards about 8 cm by 6 cm (3 ins by 2¼ ins)—for dominoes these can easily be divided in half.

Designs

1. Shapes—use the shapes shown on the previous page by tracing over them.
2. Pictures—the pictures shown on the next few pages will give you some ideas.
3. Numbers—use only the numbers from 0 to 10 to begin with and write them out clearly.
4. Letters—use lower-case (i.e. small) letters only to begin with, and write them out clearly and boldly.
5. Words (for playing snap)—choose words that your child is learning and use lower-case letters throughout.

Colour Coding

To help your child match up the cards you could use colour coding. For example, make all the cards in one set the same colour, and all the cards in another set a different colour.

Other Uses

When you are making cards for a particular game think of other ways in which they can be used. For example, choose pictures that can be grouped together, such as shoes and socks or hats and coats. Or draw objects that illustrate the words your child is learning to read.

All of the games mentioned on the next four pages can be played using either shape, picture, number or letter cards.

Card games

Pairs

Make a set of 12 pairs of cards (24 cards in all). Scatter them face-downwards on the table.

To play—the first player turns over any two cards. If they are a pair the player picks them up and keeps them. If not, the player must turn them face-downwards again, leaving them in the same position (and trying to remember what was on them). Then it is the turn of the next player. The winner is the person to collect the most pairs.

For young children: To introduce the game to a young child, use only three pairs (six cards) to begin with and gradually increase the number of pairs.

Lotto

This game is for two players. Make 12 pairs of cards (24 in all). Put one card from each pair in a box and shake them up. Lay six of the other cards face up in front of each player.

To play—each player in turn chooses a card from the box. If the card they have chosen matches one of the cards in front of them they place it on top of the correct card. If not, the card is returned to the box. The winner is the first person to cover their six cards.

Happy Families

Make 24 cards—six sets with four identical cards in each set. Shuffle the cards and deal six to each player. Stack the remainder face-down between the players. The object is to collect complete sets of four identical cards.

To play—the first player asks another player for a card (to match one that they hold in their hand). For example, one player could ask another one for a card with a cat on it.

If the other player has the card they must hand it over immediately to the first player, who then has another turn. If the other player doesn't have the card, the first player takes a card from the stack in the centre and the turn passes to the next player. When a player completes a set, they should place it on the table in front of them.

The game continues until all the sets have been collected. The winner is the player with the largest number of sets.

Snap

Make 24 cards—six sets with four identical cards in each set. Shuffle the cards and deal them all out amongst the players, face-downwards so that the players do not know what cards they have.

To play—each player in turn takes a card from the top of their pack and places it face-up on the table. When two identical cards appear together both players must shout 'snap'. The first player to call out wins all the cards that have been put down so far and adds them to the bottom of their own pile.

The winner is either the player who has the most cards at the end of the game, or the one who wins all the cards.

Note: For games of Snap or Happy Families involving more than two players, you may wish to make more than six sets of cards.

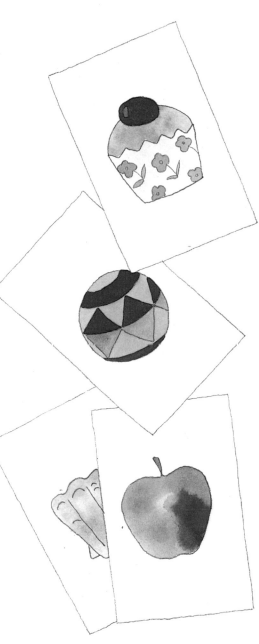

The meaning of numbers

Make use of everyday opportunities to help your child to understand the meaning of numbers and how they are used.

For example, when laying the table you could:

1 Talk about what 'one' represents, such as 'One knife for Mummy', 'One knife for Daddy', and so on.

2 Compare stacks of plates of different sizes.

3 Show how numbers of objects have nothing to do with size of objects. For example, is four of something always the same size? Try carrying in four teaspoons and then four chairs.

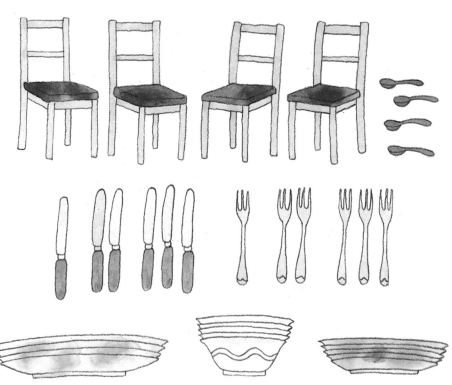

Counting

1 Count out piles of buttons, rice, raisins or similar objects into styrofoam trays or pots.

2 Make hand and foot prints with paints and count the numbers of fingers and toes.

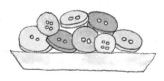

3 Make 'counting pictures', for example, lights on a Christmas tree, peas in a pod, a flock of birds, eggs in a nest, wheels on a train.

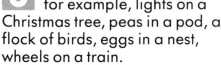

5 Place three buttons on a table. Ask your child to put three other objects next to them. Repeat this project with all the numbers that your child is learning.

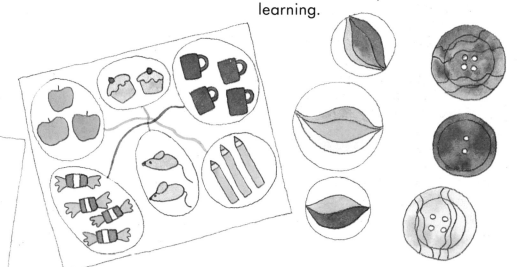

4 Draw different groups of objects on a large sheet of paper and put a circle around each group. Join the groups that have the same number of objects in them with a coloured line.

Picture Chart

Count all the people or vehicles passing your window during the space of, say, five or ten minutes. Draw a picture chart to show how many there were of each kind.

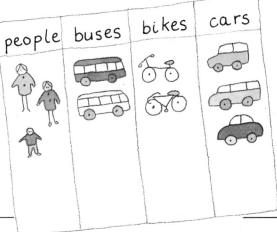

Jumping Jack

If you have a stringed puppet or a doll you could draw a picture of a wide river with stepping stones across it. Make the puppet 'jump' from stone to stone and count the jumps.

Or, put some newspaper stepping stones on the floor so that your child can count their own jumps.

More or Less

Introduce the words 'more' and 'less'.

1 Place some buttons in a row of styrofoam trays in numerical sequence, i.e. one button in the first tray, two in the second, three in the third, etc.

By pointing to each tray from left to right, show how there is one more button in each tray. Then do the same thing but in the reverse sequence. (If you don't have enough buttons use nuts or pebbles or something similar.)

2 Make a selection of picture cards showing groups of objects from one to four. These can be arranged in various ways, showing cards going from low numbers to high, from high to low, or different groups of the same numbers.

3 Draw the outlines of two groups of objects with a different number of objects in each group. Help your child to colour in, say, the larger group in red and the smaller in blue.

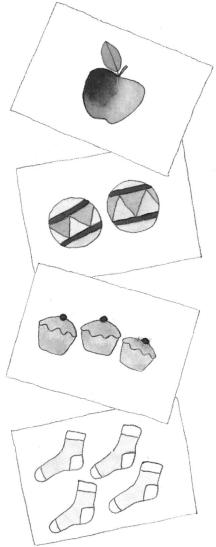

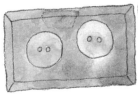

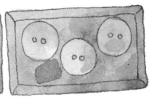

Number games

Number Dominoes

Make a set of domino cards following the sequence shown below. Use dots to represent the numbers and only do the numbers from one to six. Make your cards more interesting by making a picture out of the dots, like the butterfly shown here.

To play — place all dominoes face down on one side of the table. Each player takes eight dominoes. The first player lays down one domino face up. If the second player has a matching domino they put that domino down. If not, they take a domino from the spare pile. The winner is the first to play all their dominoes.

1	1		1	2		1	3		1	4		1	5		1	6
2	2		2	3		2	4		2	5		2	6
			3	3		3	4		3	5		3	6
						4	4		4	5		4	6
									5	5		5	6
												6	6

Jigsaw Game

Mount six pictures onto thick card, then divide each picture into six pieces. Clearly number each piece from one to six—using dots not figures. Make a dice (see page 27). For two players use two of the pictures, for three players use three pictures, and so on.

Show each player one completed jigsaw picture, then jumble up all the pieces and place them all face upwards in the middle of the table. The aim is for the players to collect the six pieces required to complete their picture.

To play—each player in turn shakes the dice and finds the piece from his or her picture that corresponds to the number shown on the dice. The winner is the first person to complete a picture.

Board games

Make some simple board games. They can represent either:

1 A single winding track, such as the route home from school, a treasure hunt, or a maze.

2 Parallel tracks, such as a race track or railway lines.

3 Adjacent squares, such as a 'snakes and ladders' game.

Keep the games fairly simple and try to work in jokes,

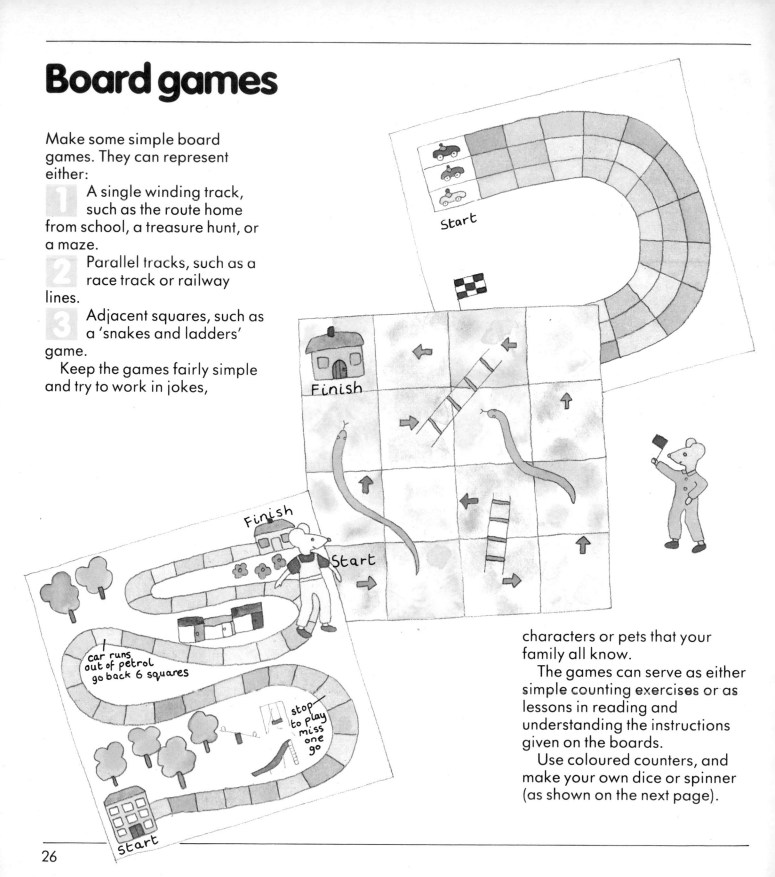

Start

Finish

Finish

Start

car runs out of petrol go back 6 squares

stop to play miss one go

Start

characters or pets that your family all know.

The games can serve as either simple counting exercises or as lessons in reading and understanding the instructions given on the boards.

Use coloured counters, and make your own dice or spinner (as shown on the next page).

Making dice and spinners

To Make a Dice

Trace around the diagram shown here. Cut out this shape from firm card and colour in the dots in the sequence shown.

Fold along all the dotted lines. Then glue the flaps to the sides with the matching letters—in alphabetical order—for example, flap 'a' to side 'a' and so on.

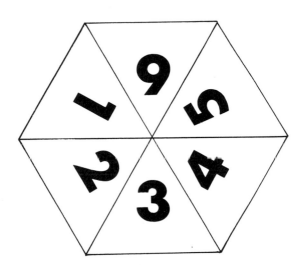

To Make a Spinner

Trace around the diagram shown here. Cut the hexagon shape from thick card. Draw on the lines and the numbers (or use dots instead of numbers). Push a cocktail stick or a pencil with a sharp point through the centre of the hexagon and spin it between thumb and forefinger.

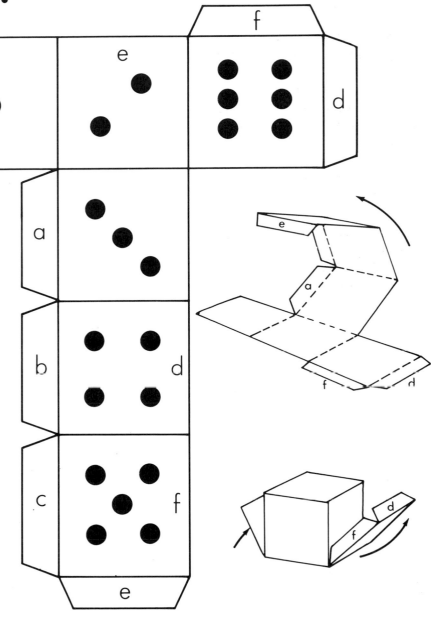

Number rhymes

The following number rhymes are just a few of the many that can be found in children's books. Where you can, act them out with your fingers while saying them.

You could also make up your own rhymes, for example:

1 2 3 4 Stephen's on the
    kitchen floor,
5 6 7 8 counting biscuits on
    his plate.

Or, using the tune of 'Ten Green Bottles' in other ways, for example:

There are five shiny teaspoons
    on the draining board,
Five shiny teaspoons on the
    draining board,
And if one shiny teaspoon is
    put into the drawer,
There are four shiny teaspoons
    on the draining board . . . .
And so on.

Buckle My Shoe
One, two, buckle my shoe,
Three, four, knock at the door,
Five, six, pick up sticks,
Seven, eight, shut the gate,
Nine, ten, a big fat hen.

(Traditional)

Who's Who?
Two legs sat upon three legs,
With one leg in his lap,
In comes four legs,
And runs away with one leg,
Up jumps two legs,
Catches up three legs,
Throws it after four legs,
And makes him bring back one leg.

(Traditional)

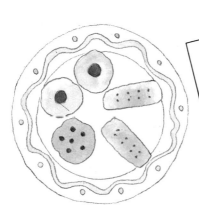

The Poor Widow
Here's to the poor widow from
    Babylon,
With six poor children all alone.
One can bake and one can brew,
One can shape and one can sew,
One can sit at the fire and spin,
One can bake a cake for the king.
Come choose you east, come choose
    you west,
Come choose the one that you
    love best.

(Traditional)

Ten Little Soldiers

Ten little soldiers
    Standing in a line,
One toddled home,
    And then there were nine.

Nine little soldiers
    Swinging on a gate,
One tumbled off,
    And then there were eight.

Eight little soldiers,
    Tried to fly to heaven,
One lost his wings,
    And then there were seven.

(and so on, through the next verses)
Seven . . . Playing silly tricks,
    One broke his neck,
Six . . . . . . Kicking all alive,
    One went to bed,
Five . . . . On a cellar door,
    One tumbled in,
Four . . . . Out on a spree,
    One got sick,
Three . . . . Out in a canoe,
    One tumbled overboard,
Two . . . . Fooling with a gun,
    One shot the other,

One little soldier,
    With his little wife,
Lived in a castle,
    The rest of his life.

(Traditional)

How Many?
3 young rats with black felt
    hats,
3 young ducks with white straw
    hats,
3 young dogs with curling
    tails,
3 young cats with demi-veils,
Went out to walk with 2 young
    pigs,
In satin vests and sorrel wigs,
But suddenly it chanced to rain,
And so they all went home again.

(Traditional)

Recognizing and writing numbers

When your child seems to have a fairly clear idea of what numbers mean, you could help him or her to learn the symbols that represent the numbers.

Draw out the numbers your child knows in dotted lines so they can be traced over.

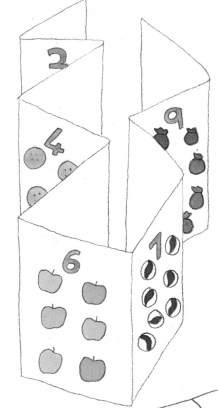

Number Jigsaws
Cut out ten cards. Write one of the numbers from one to ten on the top of each card and glue on or draw a group of simple objects of the same number below it.

Cut a wavy line between the number and picture on each card. Make sure the line is different for each one, to help your child match up the right picture with the right number.

Number Frieze
Fold up a long piece of paper, or stick a number of sheets together to make a frieze. Write the numbers from one to ten on the top of each sheet or folded section. Then stick pictures (or the objects themselves if they are light enough) underneath the numbers to illustrate each one.

Number Worm
Take a piece of thick card and draw a long wavy worm on it. Split the worm into ten segments and write the numbers from one to ten on each segment with the equivalent number of dots beside each number.

As you cut the segments up, make the curves of each cut different, so that the worm can only be reassembled with the numbers in the correct order.

Use practical examples to illustrate numbers to your child and, whenever possible, use real objects rather than pictures. For example:

Counting

1 'Let's do up your buttons—one, two, three . . .'

2 'How many people will be eating dinner?' . . . 'Here are all the knives and forks' . . . 'How many forks have you got . . . can you give everyone a fork?' . . . 'How many knives have you got . . . can you give everyone a knife?' . . . and so on, with spoons and dishes.

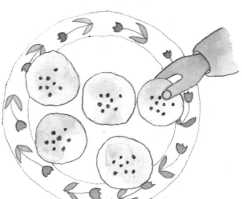

Adding On

1 'Here are two buttons . . . here are two more . . . how many are there now?'

2 'I have three pencils . . . pass me one more pencil . . . how many do I have now?'

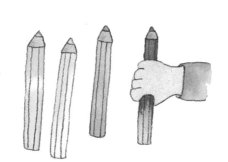

Taking Away

1 'There are five biscuits on this plate. You eat one. How many are there now?'

2 'You have three dolls. If you give one doll to me, how many do you have left?'

Sharing

'Here are four cakes. How many people are there in the room? Will they each be able to have a cake?'

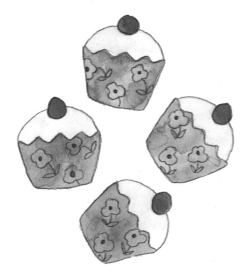

Shopping Games

You can buy and sell items around the house, such as toys, clothes or groceries, using buttons, counters or beans as money. Let one button represent one unit of money, such as one penny, so that there is no need to give change.

You could also collect a tin full of real pennies and play with them in the same way.

Measuring

Introduce these words wherever possible, and make some cards that you can ask questions about to help to illustrate their meaning: high—highest, low—lowest, big—biggest, small—smallest, many, most, less.

Who is the smallest?

Which monster has the most legs?

Which kite is flying the highest?

Which animal is the biggest?

Make a Simple Ruler

Cut out a strip of strong card about 3 cm by 20 cm and section off the card in 1 cm units along the ruler. (NB: Do not make your ruler in inches, as your child will be using the metric system in school.)

Use the ruler to measure books, doors, tables and other objects around the house.

| 1 | 2 | 3 | 4 | 5 | 6 | 7 | 8 | 9 | 10 | 11 | 12 | 13 | 14 | 15 | 16 | 17 | 18 | 19 | 20 |